Do I Have to Say Hello?

BLUE RIDER PRESS   *New York*

Do I Have to Say Hello?

Aunt Delia's Manners Quiz for Kids and Their Grownups

Delia Ephron

with drawings by
Edward Koren

blue
rider
press

An imprint of Penguin Random House LLC
375 Hudson Street
New York, New York 10014

Text copyright © 1989, 2015 by Delia Ephron
Illustrations copyright © 1989, 2015 by Edward Koren
Originally published by Viking Penguin Inc.

Library of Congress Cataloging-in-Publication Data

Ephron, Delia, author.
    Do I have to say hello? : aunt Delia's manners quiz for kids and their grownups / Delia Ephron ; with drawings by Edward Koren.
        p.   cm.
    Originally published: New York, N.Y. : Viking, 1989.
    ISBN 978-1-101-98307-2
1. Etiquette for children and teenagers—Juvenile humor.   I. Koren, Edward, illustrator.   II. Title.
    BJ1857.C5E64   2015   2015017174
    395.122—dc23

Printed in the United States of America
3   5   7   9   10   8   6   4   2

BOOK DESIGN BY NICOLE LAROCHE

Lucky you. It's from Aunt Delia.

How do you reply?

"Go jump in the lake."

"I hate tests."

"Okay, but I'm bringing forty friends. You'd better have food."

"I don't really want to, but my mom wants me to."

"I'd love to, Aunt Delia. Thank you so much for asking me."

If you accepted the invitation, what do you do now?

Turn the page.

Close the book and throw it out the window.

Contents

Do I Have to Say Hello?

Table Manners

Your aunt is making dinner and she asks you to set the table.

Do you say, "I can't. I'm busy"?

Do you moan and say, "Oh, okay, but I'm so tired"?

Do you say, "Why should I have to set the table? Why doesn't Uncle Jerry? He never does anything"?

Do you say, "Sure, Aunt Delia"?

You put down place mats, plates, forks, knives, spoons, napkins, and glasses. Finally you're finished. What do you say?

"Would you like me to do anything else, Aunt Delia?"

"Okay, I did it, but next time, do it yourself."

Dinner is ready. You sit down. Where do you put your napkin?

Around your neck.

On your head.

In your lap.

Now your aunt is serving. She asks if you would like some chicken.

Do you say, "Gimme"?

Do you say, "Stick 'em up, Aunt Delia, and hand over your drumsticks"?

Do you say, "I'd like a drumstick, please"?

"What about some string beans? They're so delicious," says Aunt Delia. You hate string beans. What do you say?

"Yuck."

"Give them to Uncle Jerry. He looks like a string bean."

"No, thank you."

But suppose your aunt puts string beans on your plate without asking if you want them? What would you do then?

Say, "String beans make me puke, Aunt Delia."

Wait until she isn't looking and put a string bean up your nose.

Just ignore the string beans and hope Aunt Delia is nice enough that she won't ask you to eat just one.

Do any of these drawings show the proper way to sit while you eat?

Which of these is it okay to do while you eat dinner with your aunt and uncle?

Beat your chest and yell, "Me Tarzan."

Peel your scab.

Download six apps on Aunt Delia's phone.

Listen.

Talk.

Snore.

Which of these are not appropriate subjects for dinner table conversation?

What Aunt Delia and Uncle Jerry did at work today.

Tushies.

The dead rat in Uncle Jerry and Aunt Delia's garage.

Throw-up.

Snot.

What you want to be when you grow up.

That Aunt Delia looks about a hundred years old.

Whether you can say without making a mistake, "One smart fellow, he felt smart. Two smart fellows, they felt smart. Three smart fellows, they all felt smart."

You want another helping of corn.

Do you say, "Please pass the corn, Uncle Jerry"?

Do you say, "Yo, corn"?

Do you bang the table with your knife until Aunt Delia and Uncle Jerry ask what you want?

When your uncle passes the corn, you notice that there is just a little bit left and nobody else has had seconds yet. You are the first. What do you do?

Ask, "Does anyone else want seconds?" so that you can leave a little for other people at the table.

Say, "Aunt Delia, you didn't make enough."

Take it all.

Suppose you took it all and then as soon as you put a big forkful of corn in your mouth, Aunt Delia asks what happened at school today.

Do you wait until you're finished chewing and then tell her?

Do you answer, spraying corn across the table?

Do you open your mouth and point at what's inside so your aunt figures out you can't talk?

Uncle Jerry burps by accident.
Do you fall off your chair, laughing?
Do you keep eating, pretending you don't think it's funny because you don't
   want to embarrass Uncle Jerry?

You burp by accident.
Do you fall off your chair, laughing?
Do you say, "Excuse me"?

Uh-oh, you have to sneeze.

Do you cover your mouth and nose with your napkin and then do it?

Do you aim straight at the chicken and then do it?

Do you say, "Surprise, Uncle Jerry," and do it in his face?

Uh-oh, Uncle Jerry has to sneeze.

Do you duck?

Do you say, "God bless you, Uncle Jerry"?

Do you chant, "Do it again, do it again. I like it, I like it"?

You are finished eating. What do you do with your knife and fork?

Put them in your hair as if they were barrettes.

Stab your leftover meat with them so they poke up like flagpoles.

Place them lying down, side by side, on the plate.

What is the proper way to wipe your mouth?

With your hand.

With your T-shirt.

With your napkin.

What is the proper way to inform your aunt and uncle that you are finished and would like to leave the table?

A burp.

"May I please be excused?"

"See ya."

What do you do with your plate?

Take it into the kitchen.

Put it under your chair.

Toss it like a Frisbee out the window.

The Sharing Chart

Select the drawings in which you are sharing generously with your friend.

CHIPS

WATERMELON

SPINACH

Birthday Party Manners

It's your birthday today. You are having a big party and are so excited. Your friend Polly arrives. What's the first thing you say to her?

"What did you bring me?"

"Hi, Polly. I'm so glad you could come."

"Who invited you? There must be some mistake."

What's the first thing you say to the birthday girl?

"Happy birthday."

"My mother made me come."

"Where's the food?"

Polly doesn't go to your school. She doesn't know anyone else at the party.

Do you say, "Polly, these are my friends Naomi and Max. Naomi and Max, this is Polly"?

Do you say, "Good luck trying to meet kids"?

Do you say, "Naomi and Max, this is poor, pitiful Polly. She doesn't have any friends"?

All the guests are here. It's time for Uncle Jerry to do his magic tricks. Everyone has to sit on the grass and be quiet. Which is the best way to ask your guests to do this?

Call out, "Okay, everyone. Time for the magic show. Please sit on the grass and be quiet."

Shout, "Sit down and shut up."

Everyone sits down for the show. When you go to take your seat, you discover that there's no room for you in the front row.

Do you sit in the back row?

Do you say, "You have to sit in the back, Naomi," and take her seat?

Do you cry?

Now it gets tricky. Suppose you told Naomi to sit in the back and she refused. What would you do then?

Stamp your foot and shout, "I'M THE BIRTHDAY GIRL. IT'S MY DAY. EVERYONE MUST DO AS I SAY."

Pull Naomi's hair.

Say, "Oh, okay," and sit in the back.

Uncle Jerry needs a helper for his trick where he puts an egg in a hat and pulls out a roast chicken. He asks for a volunteer.

Do you raise your hand?

Do you say, "Uncle Jerry, may I please speak to you privately?" and explain that if he expects to get a cupcake, he'd better make *you* the magician's helper?

Do you shout, "The birthday girl gets to choose," and then choose yourself?

Which guests are behaving badly during the show?

Guest Bonus Question

When the magic show is over, what do you do?
Applaud.
Boo.
Throw things.

It's time to choose teams for the relay race. Polly doesn't want to play because she's shy.

Do you ignore her?

Do you chant, "Polly's a party pooper, Polly's a party pooper"?

Do you say, "Polly, I'd really like it if you'd play. You can be on my team. I'll show you how"?

You get chosen for a team you don't want to be on. What do you do?
    Cry.
    Be a good sport and join the team.
    Take your birthday present back.

Your team wins! Aunt Delia hands out all the prizes and discovers that she's one prize short. Either you or Polly isn't going to get one.

Do you say, "Give it to Polly, Aunt Delia. I'm getting lots of presents today"?

Do you say, "I want it. It's my birthday"?

Do you burst into tears and cry until Polly feels so bad that she tells Aunt Delia to give the prize to you?

Do you throw the prize in the bushes so no one gets it?

Which of these things is it okay for the birthday girl to say while she hands out cupcakes?

"Raise your hand if you think I'm pretty."

"Sit down and shut up."

"Who wants one with pink frosting?"

"I'm giving chocolate ice cream to kids I really, really like, and vanilla to those I only sort of like."

Do any of these drawings show the proper thing to do with your cup when you are finished with your juice?

Birthday Present Time

Everyone is sitting around watching you open presents except Max, who is busy learning a magic trick from your Uncle Jerry.

Do you start unwrapping presents even though he's not paying attention?

Do you shout, "Max, watch me"?

Do you start crying and tell Uncle Jerry he's ruining your party by taking all your friends away?

The first present you open is just what you've always wanted.

Do you say, "Thank you, Jacob, this is just what I've always wanted"?

Do you throw it down and start opening the next one?

Do you say, "Oh, I love this. How much did it cost"?

Suppose you asked how much it cost and Jacob said, "Fifteen dollars."
What would you say then?

"Cheapo."

"Wow!"

Your aunt asks to speak to you privately and says it's not good manners to ask the price of presents. "How much it costs doesn't matter," says Aunt Delia. "It's the thought that counts."

Do you say, "Mind your own business, Aunt Delia"?

Do you say to Jacob, "That was a good thought even if it was a cheap one"?

Do you say no more to Jacob about the cost of his present and not ask the cost of any other presents either?

Guest Bonus Question

When the birthday girl opens your present and thanks you, what do you say?

"Duh."

"Don't thank me, thank my mom. She picked it out."

"We bought it 'cause it had free shipping."

"You're welcome."

Your second present is a book that you have already read.

Do you say, "Thank you, Anna"?

Do you say, "I've already read this"?

Do you say, "Who wants this?" and give it to a kid who raises his hand?

Your next present is a very funny-looking sweater that you would never wear.

Do you say, "Thank you very much, Emily"?

Do you say, "Can you take this back? Here's what I really want. A crystal-making kit"?

Do you say, "This is the most beautiful sweater I have ever seen. I will treasure it always"?

Do you say, "This is the ugliest sweater I have ever seen. Mom will take it to Goodwill"?

Do you burst out laughing?

Do you pretend to throw up?

After unwrapping all the presents, the party's over. Polly's mom is the first to arrive. Aunt Delia says, "You remember Polly's mom, don't you, dear?" What do you say?

"Don't shake my hand, it's sweaty."

"Hello. It's very nice to see you again."

"Who's Polly?"

Polly says, "Thank you for having me."

Do you say, "Thank you for coming"?

Do you say, "Well, everyone makes mistakes"?

Do you say, "You were very fortunate to have been invited to my party. I may consider inviting you again, but I'm not sure. Perhaps if you text me around this time next year, you might be lucky enough to be on the guest list. Waka waka"?

Tricky Question 1

Who has the butter knife?

Car Manners

Uncle Jerry is taking you and your cousin Matt to the movies.

"Tell us a story," you say to Uncle Jerry.

"Okay," says Uncle Jerry. "I'll tell you a story, but you have to find the crazy parts.

"Once upon a time, your Uncle Jerry was taking you and Matt to the movies. You and Matt got into an argument. 'I want to sit in front!' 'No, me!' Uncle Jerry suggested that the best way to settle the argument was for you and Matt to hit each other. So after you slugged Matt and he slugged you, and Uncle Jerry congratulated you on being so well-behaved, you both got in the backseat and immediately unfastened your seat belts. Then you rolled down the window and stuck your heads out to say hi to drivers passing by. 'Good move,' said Uncle Jerry. 'I know Aunt Delia thinks that the safest way to ride is with your head out the window.'

"The traffic suddenly got terrible. Bumper-to-bumper. To help Uncle Jerry concentrate, you grabbed his glasses. 'Thanks,' said Uncle Jerry. Then you put your hands over his eyes and said, 'Guess who?'

"'Oh boy, now I can really see clearly,' said Uncle Jerry.

"As the car crept along, you saw the reason for the jam—a big truck stuck in the road. You stood on the seat to get a better view. 'Stand on tiptoe,' said Uncle Jerry. 'That way, if I stop short, you won't get hurt.'

"'I'm starved, Uncle Jerry,' you said. 'Gimme a banana.'

"'I love it when you're polite,' said Uncle Jerry. He took both hands off the wheel to get one for you. 'The car will drive itself,' said Uncle Jerry.

"You unpeeled the banana and dropped the peel on the floor because you didn't want to get the plastic garbage bag dirty. Some banana fell in your lap by accident. 'What do I do with this?' you asked Uncle Jerry. 'Squash it into the seat next to me,' said Uncle Jerry. 'Squash it and smear it. That's the most considerate thing to do because then Aunt Delia will get banana on her pants. Aunt Delia loves banana stains.'

"'I want juice now. Get it for me or else,' you said to Uncle Jerry.

"'What a sweet way to ask,' said Uncle Jerry, handing you a box of apple juice.

"You drank it quickly and threw the box out the window. 'Good for you,' said Uncle Jerry. 'Boxes and flowers look pretty together, and you don't want to get the plastic garbage bag dirty.'

"Then you discovered that Matt's foot was on your side of the seat. 'Kick him,' said Uncle Jerry. 'If someone is on your side, the best thing to do is give him a big fat kick.' So you kicked Matt, and Uncle Jerry said, 'Okay, Matt, kick him back.' Matt did.

"'Wasn't that a smart way to solve the problem?' asked Uncle Jerry.

"'Yes, we feel so grown up,' said you and Matt together.

"'Aunt Delia will be proud of you for kicking,' said Uncle Jerry.

"He parked the car, you fastened your seat belt, and got out. The end.

"I hope you liked that story," says Uncle Jerry. Then he gives you a bonus question.

Put these three sentences in the order in which they should take place.

a) Throw up.

b) Get out of the car.

c) Ask Uncle Jerry to pull over.

Beach Manners

Aunt Delia unpacks the car: five towels, a blanket, a cooler, one pail,
a shovel, her tote bag, and a beach umbrella. She asks you to help carry
something.

Do you say, "Sure, Aunt Delia"?

Do you say, "I'm too weak"?

Do you stop a man passing by and say, "Excuse me, but my aunt thinks you look
   like Luke Skywalker. Would you help carry her stuff"?

The beach is very crowded. You'll have enough room to put down your
towels if you can get one family to move a little bit to the left. What would
be the polite way to accomplish this?

Ask them, "Would you mind moving over a little to the left?"

Kick sand on them from the right.

Say, "Move it. What are you trying to do—hog the place?"

Which of these things should sand be used for?

Building sand castles.

Burying Aunt Delia.

Sprinkling on sandwiches.

Throwing.

Which of these things is it okay to say in a loud voice at the beach?

"Oh, it's so beautiful here."

"The sand in my suit is making my butt itch."

"Why is that man so fat?"

"Boy, did that bathroom smell."

"Aunt Delia, that woman isn't wearing a top."

"Sharks! Sharks!"

You see a kid building a sand castle. You want to help.

Do you tell him your name and ask, "May I please help"?

Do you knock his sand castle over and then say, "Awww, look what happened to your sand castle. You probably need help building another"?

Do you say, "What ugly turrets. I'll fix them"?

Do you say, "I'm a much better sand castle builder than you are. Do you want to see how much better I can make this?"

There is a girl playing in the water. What is a good thing to say if you want to make friends with her?

"Hi. Do you want to play?"

"My aunt and uncle are very rich and I'm going to inherit all their money."

"You probably want to be my friend because I've met Beyoncé."

"You probably don't want to be my friend, but in case you do, here's my name."

Beach Towel Bonus Questions

Yes or no answers only.

It is a good idea to wave your beach towel in the air so sand flies into the food.

It is a good idea to wave your beach towel in the air so sand flies into Aunt Delia's face.

People love it when you snap a wet towel at them.

Aunt Delia will love it if you turn all your sand crabs loose on her towel.

Beach towels make good rafts.

When you go home, you should leave your towel on the sand to be used by the next person who comes to the beach.

Aunt Delia gasps, "Oh my goodness, I forgot to put sunblock on you. Come here."

Do you say, "No"?

Do you let Aunt Delia cover you with lotion?

Do you say, "Too late," and jump in the water?

After lunch, what do you do with the garbage?

See if it floats.

Throw it in the trash can.

Sit on it.

Now it's time to go home. Aunt Delia asks you to help carry things to the car.

Do you say, "I'd love to. Thank you, thank you, thank you, I had so much fun"?

Do you say, "I can't. There's sand between my toes"?

Do you shout, "Bathing beauty contest! Winner gets to help my aunt"?

The Eating Chart

Which of these foods are you eating properly?

PEAS

MASHED POTATOES

CHEERIOS

CHIPS

JELL-O

SPAGHETTI

OATMEAL RAISIN COOKIE

ICE CREAM

TORTILLA CHIPS

Visiting Manners

Uncle Jerry is taking you to meet his friends Marco and Maria Madrid.
"Do I have to say hello?" you ask Aunt Delia. What does Aunt
Delia say?
"Yes."
"No. Just stand on your head and wave your legs."

When the Madrids answer the door, Uncle Jerry says, "Maria, Marco,
I'd like you to meet my nephew, whom I've told you so much about."
Do you say, "What smells"?
Do you say, "Hello, Maria," and shake her hand and then do the same
    with Marco?
Do you look at your shoes?
Do you mumble, "Hi," and pick your nose?
Do you cling to your uncle and say, "I want to go home"?

Maria asks, "Are you hungry? Would you like something to eat?"

Do you say, "Yes, please"?

Do you pull up your shirt, point to your stomach, and say, "Belly wants cookie"?

Do you say, "You bet your fat bottom"?

"Seaweed crunchies, Goldfish, or homemade chocolate chip cookies—which would you like?" asks Maria.

Do you say, "Seaweed is vomitrocious"?

Do you say, "Are there nuts in the cookies or are the only nuts in this house you and Marco"?

Do you say, "I'd like a cookie, please"?

Do you say, "I'll grunt once for seaweed, twice for Goldfish, and three times for chocolate chip"?

After you eat a cookie, you are thirsty. What do you do?

Say, "May I please have something to drink?"

Say really loudly, "Boy, I sure am thirsty," and hope someone gets the message.

Walk into the kitchen, open the refrigerator, take out a carton of lemonade, and start drinking.

Say, "Marco and Maria, there are two kinds of people in this world. People who offer their guests something to drink and people who let their guests die of thirst. Which kind are you?"

While you all sit around the table, what would be a good way to start a conversation with Marco?

"Do you wear false teeth?"

"What's your favorite baseball team?"

"May I please see your pajamas?"

"Uncle Jerry's underpants are purple."

Conversation Bonus Question

Let's say you asked Marco about his favorite baseball team and he said, "I don't like any of them." What would be a good way to change the subject?

"Have you ever considered going on a diet?"

"What was your favorite book when you were a kid?"

"Your nose is peeling."

After discussing gray parrots, elephants, and dinosaurs with Marco, what would be a good way to start a conversation with Maria?

"Tell me, Maria, do you get much earwax?"

"Have you ever eaten a fly?"

"Seen any good movies lately?"

"How much did your house cost?"

"What color is your tongue?"

Now you're bored. Uncle Jerry and the Madrids are discussing income tax deductions. What should you do?

Climb to the top of the china cabinet.

Throw a tantrum on the rug.

Torture Maria's beloved dog, Daisy.

Read.

Uncle Jerry finally says it's time to leave. "Aunt Delia will be wondering what happened to us."

Do you say, "Good-bye. It was very nice to meet you"?

Do you shout, "Hurray, I'm free"?

Do you suck your thumb and just stand there?

Do you say, "Good-bye, Madrids. You have a very weird name, and I hope I never see you again"?

Asking Manners

Your friend Molly asks you to sleep over. You have to get permission from Aunt Delia. In which of these conversations are you asking politely?

"Aunt Delia, may I please sleep at
    Molly's?"
"Yes, dear."
"Thank you."

"Aunt Delia, may I please sleep at
    Molly's?"
"It's a school night."
"If I promise to do all my homework
    before I go, and go to sleep at nine
    o'clock, may I do it just this once?"
"All right, if you promise."

"I'm sleeping at Molly's, Aunt Delia, and I told her you'd take me."
"What? It's out of the question. First of all, you didn't ask permission. Second,
    it's a school night."
"Molly said you should get me there by six o' clock."
"I said you're not going."
"Here are the car keys, Aunt Delia. Get in and start driving."

"Aunt Delia, I promised Molly I'd sleep over."

"I'm sorry, you can't—it's a school night."

"But I promised."

"You should have asked me first."

"But you weren't here."

"Then you should have told Molly that you couldn't give her an answer until I got home."

"But Molly's expecting me, her mom's expecting me, they made a special chocolate cake in honor of my arrival. I make them happy. I cheer them up. You'll ruin their whole day if you don't let me go. Is that what you want?"

"I have to sleep over at Molly's tonight because it's our homework assignment."

"Your homework assignment?"

"Yes. And if I don't do it, I'll fail."

"May I please sleep at Molly's?"

"No."

"Okay."

"Please, beautiful aunt, gorgeous aunt, sweetest aunt, aunt whom I love more than anything in the world, may I please sleep at Molly's?"

"No. It's a school night."

"I hate you."

"Aunt Delia, say, 'Y.'"
"Y."
"Now say, 'E.'"
"E."
Now say, 'S.'"
"S."
"Thanks, Aunt Delia. Molly, Aunt Delia says I can sleep over."

Soccer Manners

Your team, the Scorpions, is playing the Rebels. It's your turn to kick off.
You walk into the center of the field. What do you do?

Check to see if your shoes are tied.

Kiss the referee.

Gel your hair.

Uncle Jerry and Aunt Delia are standing on the sidelines. What does Uncle
Jerry shout when you get the ball?

"You forgot to make your bed and you can't pass until you do."

"Go, go, go, go, go, go, go!!!!!!"

"Remind me to buy toilet paper on the way home."

The ball lands out-of-bounds. What do you do next?

Throw it over your head back to your team.

Kick it into the parking lot.

Toss it to the crowd.

You are running toward the goal, your teammate passes you the ball. You trap it, dribble, and shoot. It goes in! You think you scored but the referee calls offsides. What do you do?

Walk back quietly and take your position.

Lie on top of the ball in the goal and refuse to get up.

Grab the linesman's flag and give it to Aunt Delia to fan herself.

Now you're playing defense. The forward is running with the ball, about to shoot. You slide and get the ball, the forward falls over you, and the referee calls a penalty. What do you do?

Nothing.

Scream, "I got the ball first," and keep screaming until the coach carries you off the field.

Get on your knees and pray while the player takes his penalty kick.

Tell your goalie, "Save it or you're never sitting at our lunch table again."

Uncle Jerry thinks you got the ball, too. What does he do?

Nothing.

Yells mean things at the referee.

Jumps on the other kid's dad and wrestles him to the ground.

Starts crying and has to be comforted by Aunt Delia.

Uh-oh, a bad slide tackle. You get a legful of cleats. What does Aunt Delia do?

Rushes onto the field and kisses your boo-boo.

Keeps calm, and lets the coach figure out how serious it is.

Finds the other player's mom and screams at her.

Eats all the other team's orange slices.

You want to play up front and your coach says, "Sorry, mate, you're playing left-back." What do you say?

"Okay, Coach, got it."

"My feet don't work at left-back, they only work as forward."

"My Uncle Jerry says that if you don't let me play forward, he'll have you fired."

Let's say your sister's playing goalie on her team, the Ghosts.
A midfielder hits a long shot her way, she dives for it and puts her
glove up to stop it, but it zips by into the net. The other team
scores. What does she do?

Brushes her teeth.

Picks up the ball and throws it to the referee.

Shouts, "It's not fair. The sun was in my eyes."

Runs off the field, crying.

What does Uncle Jerry say when your sister doesn't block the shot?

"Good try."

"You blew it."

"If you'd made your bed, that wouldn't have happened."

"I was going to take you for pizza, but now I won't."

The game's tied. Things are tense. In stoppage time, you score the winning goal. The ref signals the end of the game. Your team, the Scorpions, wins. What do you do?

Dance around the Rebels' goalie, "I'm the greatest and you're not."

Fart.

Shout, "Everyone shut up, I'm making a speech. I love my Aunt Delia and Uncle Jerry, and I owe everything to them."

Stand on your hands and sing "The Star-Spangled Banner."

Slap the Rebels' hands and congratulate them on a good game.

Referee Bonus Question

Which of these things is it okay for Uncle Jerry to say to the referee?

"If my nephew's team wins, I'll buy you a car."

"Thank you for officiating."

Respect Yourself Manners

Which of these are good things to say before or after karate?

I am brave.

I am strong.

I am bananas.

I choose friends who accept me as I am.

I choose friends who have trampolines.

I choose friends who live in Detroit.

I am willing to fail in order to succeed.

I am willing to eat worms in order to succeed.

The only person I have control over is my Aunt Delia.

The only person I have control over is me.

I am kind and friendly.

No chocolate chip cookies for you.

I believe in my dreams.

I believe in my belly.

I choose to be a good person.

I choose to pinch my brother.

I choose to put Legos in my sister's bed.

I choose to smell.

I choose to be a walrus.

Tricky Question 2

How do you cut your meat?
With scissors.
With a knife.
With a saw.

Restaurant Manners

Aunt Delia and Uncle Jerry are taking you to Caffè Italiano, a very fancy restaurant. You are all dressed up. When you walk in, the maître d' asks, "Do you have a reservation?" "Yes," says Uncle Jerry. "Kass, for three." The maître d' shows you to your table. What do you do?

Refuse to sit down unless you can sit next to Aunt Delia.

Sit down and put your napkin in your lap.

Ask the maître d' if the plants are real.

You read the menu and discover that you don't know what half the things are. Besides, the restaurant doesn't have pizza. Oh, no! What do you say?

"There's nothing here I want to eat."

"They don't have pizza, so I guess I'll have squid."

"Aunt Delia, I'm not sure what I want. Could you please help me pick?"

Aunt Delia suggests that you would like either the ravioli in tomato sauce with mushrooms or the spaghetti with shrimp. The waiter comes to take your order. "What would you like?" he asks.

Do you say, "Guess"?

Do you say, "I didn't ask you what you're having for dinner. I don't see why you should ask me"?

Do you say, "I'd like ravioli in tomato sauce, but no mushrooms and no cheese on top, please, and a Coke. Thank you"?

"Coke?" says Aunt Delia. "I think you should order water or juice." What do you say?

"Bor-ing."

"Dad always lets me have Coke."

"Okay, Aunt Delia."

Now it gets tricky. Suppose you answered, "Dad always lets me have Coke," but you secretly know that he doesn't. And Aunt Delia, surprised, says, "Does your dad really let you have Coke?"

Do you say, "Yes"?

Do you say, "Aunt Delia, would I lie to you? I love you so much. You are my best aunt," and give her a gigantic kiss?

Do you say, "Well, I'm not sure. I guess I'll just have cranberry juice, please"?

"Your dinner comes with soup or salad," says the waiter. "What kind of soup?" asks Aunt Delia. "Minestrone," says the waiter. What do you say?

"I'll have minestrone, please."

"I'll have the soup, because the last time I had salad, I got a stomachache."

While you are waiting for your food, what do you do?

Eat the insides of sixteen pieces of bread and announce that you're full.

Play tic-tac-toe with Uncle Jerry.

Stand on the seat and check out the people at the table next to yours.

Run from one end of the restaurant to the other, waving your napkin like a flag.

The waiter brings the soup. You are about to eat it when you notice there's a fly in it.

Do you swat it?

Do you eat it?

Do you say, "Excuse me," to the waiter, "but a fly is swimming in my soup"?

Now you have to go to the bathroom.

Do you stand on your chair and shout, "I have to pee"?

Do you say quietly to your aunt and uncle, "Excuse me, I have to go to the bathroom"?

But you can't find the bathroom. You have to ask the waiter.

Do you say, "Excuse me, would you please tell me where the restroom is"?

Do you say, "Hurry, quick. Where's the toilet? I gotta go"?

When the waiter brings your ravioli, he also puts down a little side dish of zucchini. What do you say?

"Yikes! I didn't order that."

"Eew, gross."

"Thank you."

Good grief. You take a big bite of ravioli and discover that there's
a mushroom in the tomato sauce, and you specifically asked for no
mushrooms. What do you do?

Wave frantically at the waiter and, when he comes
over, open your mouth and show him what's
inside.

Put your napkin to your mouth and, without
attracting attention, get the mushroom
out of your mouth and into your napkin.

Spit the mushroom into your juice.

It's time for dessert. "We have gelato,
tiramisu, sorbet, and chocolate cake," says the waiter.

You pick chocolate cake. "Can I have a bite?" asks Uncle Jerry.

Do you say, "Sure," and pass him your plate?

Do you say, "When I'm done, you may have what's left"?

Do you say, "Order your own"?

Do you say, "You may taste the cake but no frosting"?

You are leaving the restaurant with your aunt and uncle. Your private opinion of the food was that the ravioli tasted like rubber but that the chocolate cake was delicious. Which of these things would it be right to say?

"Thank you for taking me, Uncle Jerry."

"Those ravioli tasted like rubber."

"Get me out of here fast."

"I really loved the chocolate cake."

"My dad takes me to much nicer places that cost a lot more money."

The Noise Chart

Which noises are acceptable at the dinner table?

Thank-you Manners

The Madrids sent you a red hoodie for Christmas. Aunt Delia says that you have to write them a thank-you note. Which of these would be the most polite to send?

Dear Maria and Marco,
Thank you for the hoodie.

P.S. Aunt Delia made me write this.

Dear Maria and Marco,
Thank you very much for
the beautiful red hoodie. It fits
perfectly. I can't wait to wear it to
school. I hope you had a very merry
Christmas.

Yo, Madrids,
What's happening? How's life at
your weird old house? Do you still
have Daisy the dog or did you make
her into sausages, ha, ha, ha. By the
way, thanks.

Dear cutie pies,
I had the greatest Christmas. I got
flip-flops, a spy kit, a laser helmet,
walkie-talkies, a Pokémon tin,
sponges that turn into dinosaurs,
and an ant farm, so I don't mind at
all that you gave me that gross, ugly,
disgusting hoodie.

Dear Maria and Marco,
Thanks for whatever you gave
me. I opened my presents so fast that
all the cards got mixed up. But who
cares anyway. The whole point of
Christmas is to get a lot, and I
sure did.

School Manners

Multiple Choice Test

To describe the proper way to behave in class, complete the following sentences correctly.

As usual, you arrive in class . . .
a) wearing pajamas.
b) with a sock on your head.
c) on time.

You are chewing three pieces of bubble gum. Before taking your seat, you . . .
a) throw the gum in the wastebasket.
b) stick it under your desk.
c) offer to entertain the class by blowing a bubble while dancing the hula.

Your teacher, Mrs. Fox, asks you to pass your homework to the front of the class. You . . .

a) refuse.

b) take it out of your notebook and pass it.

c) make it into a paper airplane and send it airmail.

You want to know if there will be a spelling test today. To get Mrs. Fox's attention, you . . .

a) throw a spitball.

b) raise your hand.

c) burp.

Mrs. Fox calls on you, you ask her about the test, and she says, "Yes, we're going to have a test later, but first we are going to study great explorers. Open your book to page one hundred." What page? You didn't hear.

Do you . . .

a) shout, "What page? I didn't hear"?

b) raise your hand and wait to be called on?

c) ask a kid sitting next to you?

Mrs. Fox asks if anyone in the class knows which explorer named the Pacific Ocean. You know the answer so you . . .

a) keep it a secret.

b) shout, "Balboa."

c) shout, "I'll give you a hint—he doesn't go to this school."

d) raise your hand and wait to be called on.

Mrs. Fox calls on Zachary, who doesn't know the answer, so he guesses. "Columbus," he says. Columbus! He didn't even see the Pacific! While Mrs. Fox explains that to Zachary, you . . .

a) whisper, "Dummy," loud enough for Zachary to hear.

b) keep quiet, but raise your hand with the right answer.

c) wave your hand in Mrs. Fox's face, chanting, "I know it, I know it. Me! Me! Me!"

While Mrs. Fox mentions other explorers like Admiral Byrd, you remember that you wanted your friend Jessica to feel your muscles, so you . . .
a) decide to wait until recess to show her.
b) send her a note, "Meet me at the water fountain if you want to feel my muscles."
c) assume a muscleman pose, with arms bent, and hope she notices.

Complete this sentence correctly and you get an A.
The best place to doodle is . . .
a) on your big toe.
b) on a piece of paper.
c) on the desk.

When the principal visits your class, you should . . .
a) shout, "Hi, Princy."
b) keep doing your work quietly.
c) make smacking noises with your mouth.

Mrs. Fox puts three math problems on the board and asks you to solve them. The first one is very hard, so you . . .
a) start crying.
b) try to do your best.
c) look over your friend's shoulder and copy down his answer.

You finish early. After double-checking your work, you . . .

a) draw a picture of Mrs. Fox looking like a gorilla.

b) sit quietly until Mrs. Fox picks up the papers.

c) chant, "Done, done, done, done, done."

d) use your pencils for drumsticks and Zachary's head for a drum.

e) talk to a friend.

The bell rings. It's time to go to recess. Do you . . .

a) wait until Mrs. Fox dismisses you?

b) yell, "So long, Foxy," and race out?

c) refuse to go to recess because you love class so much?

Answer this question correctly and you get an A+.

A good present for your teacher is . . .

a) an apple.

b) a dead mouse.

The Friendship Test

Answer true or false.

If a kid in your class is fat, it's okay to call him Fatso.

If a kid in your class is skinny, it's okay to call her Noodle.

If a kid in your class has a turned-up nose, it's okay to call her Piggy.

If a kid in your class has curly hair, it's okay to call her Frizzball.

If a kid in your class is short, it's okay to call him Shrimp.

If a kid in your class wears glasses, it's okay to call him Four-eyes.

If a kid in your class has a large behind, it's okay to call him Big Tush.

The Keeping Secrets Test

On the way to recess, your friend Katie whispers that she has to speak to you privately. "Promise you won't tell?" she asks. "Yes," you say. "Are you sure? It's a secret." "Yes," you say. "I think Jason is cute," says Katie. Now what do you do?

a) Say nothing to anyone.

b) Whisper to your friend Eva, "Katie likes Jason, but don't tell, it's a secret."

c) Tell Jason, "Guess who likes you? Katie."

d) Shout, "Attention, everyone, Katie wants to marry Jason."

Now the test gets harder. Let's say that you whispered to Jason, "Guess who likes you? Katie. Do you like her?" And he said, "No way! But don't tell, it's a secret. I don't want to hurt her feelings." What do you do then?

a) Say nothing to anyone.

b) Send Katie a note that says "Drop dead" and sign it "Jason."

c) Take Katie aside and say that when someone in the class told Jason that she likes him, he said he was running away to Alaska.

Let's imagine now that it all happened differently. When you told Jason, "Guess who likes you? Katie," he smiled. "Don't tell, but I like her, too," said Jason. Then what would you do?

a) Say nothing to anyone.

b) Tell your friend Eva, "Remember I told you that Katie likes Jason? Well, he likes her, but don't tell, it's a secret."

c) Send out invitations. "You are invited to the wedding of Katie and Jason to be held next recess in front of the monkey bars. Dress casual."

Interrupting Manners

Uncle Jerry is in the bathroom and you have to ask him a question. What do you do?

Barge in and surprise him.

Yell, "Are you ever coming out?"

Yell, "Hey, pooper-man, talk to me"?

Wait until he comes out.

Aunt Delia and Uncle Jerry are drinking their morning coffee and discussing global warming. You want to tell Uncle Jerry something funny—Wayne the cat tried to sit on your head. What do you do?

Say, "Wayne sat on my head."

Say, "Excuse me, Uncle Jerry, may I please tell you something?"

Say, "I'm so interesting and I know such interesting things. Want to hear one?"

Suppose when you said, "May I please tell you something?" Uncle Jerry said, "Aunt Delia and I are talking. Not now." What would you do then?

Say, "Yes, now."

Wait patiently.

Start chanting "Dadadadadadadada" really loudly until they can't hear themselves talk and have to listen to you.

Interrupting Bonus Question

Which of these are important enough to justify interrupting Aunt Delia's telephone conversation?

"When's Uncle Jerry coming home?"

"What do I do with this booger?"

"Is it two o'clock yet?"

"I'm hungry."

"My tummy hurts."

"There's someone at the front door."

As Aunt Delia and Uncle Jerry keep chatting and you wait patiently, you notice that the heat from the toaster has set the paper towels on fire. What do you do?

Wait until they're finished talking.

Say, "I'm so interesting and I know such interesting things. Want to hear one?"

Shout, "Kitchen! Toaster! Fire! Help!"

Movie Manners

You are so excited because you are dying to see *Fish Diaries 2*. Your aunt gives you the money to buy the tickets. There is a very long line to get in.

Do you get at the back of the line and wait your turn?

Do you butt in front of the line?

Do you do cartwheels?

Do you lean against the wall and moan, "I don't want to stand in line. Will you carry me, Aunt Delia"?

What do you say to the ticket seller?

"Hi, gorgeous. I'll take two."

"May I please have two tickets—one adult, one child."

"Hello there, Muggle. My name is Harry Potter, I live at Hogwarts, and I speak Parseltongue. I'll take two free tickets—one for me and one for my Aunt Dumbledore."

At the refreshment counter, Aunt Delia gives you some more money and says that you have a choice. Either you can have popcorn and a soda or you can have a candy bar. What do you say?

"Okay, Aunt Delia."

"I want candy *and* a soda. Maia's dad lets her!"

When you order, what do you say to the girl working behind the counter?

"Two scoops of broccoli, please."

"Bonjour, babycakes. Hand over one package of Milk Duds, a Snickers bar, Junior Mints, Gummi-Bears, three Sprites, a large popcorn, and send the bill to my aunt."

"May I please have a small popcorn with butter and a Sprite?"

Candy Counter Bonus Question with Ratings

"Would you like anything else?" asks the girl. What do you say now?

    G: "No thank you. That will be all."

    PG: "Yes. A big smooch."

    PG-13: "Put your hands up and get inside the popcorn machine."

    R: "I want *you* covered with butter flavor."

As soon as you sit down in the theater, two kids want to come down your row and sit on the other side of you.

Do you stand up and let them walk by?

Do you put your legs up so they can't get past and say, "Toll bridge, twenty-five cents"?

Do you say, "Sorry, folks. These seats are saved"?

The lights are dimming. The movie's about to begin.

Do you stop talking?

Do you keep talking?

Do you shout, "Quiet, everyone. Movie time"?

Uh-oh, you're confused. You can't figure out why Diandra, the blowfish, is hiding in the seaweed and whether that octopus, José, is good or bad.

Do you shout, "I'm so mixed up"?

Do you whisper to your aunt, "Why is she in the seaweed, and is he a good guy"?

You just realized who that shark in the movie reminds you of—Marco Madrid.

Do you tell your aunt right now?

Do you wait until the movie's over?

Do you shout, "Hey, that shark looks like a friend of mine"?

Let's say that you told your aunt right away and the man sitting behind you said, "Quiet, please."

Do you say, "I'm sorry," and stop talking?

Do you say, "Make me"?

You don't want any more popcorn, but there is still some left. What are you going to do with it?

G: Put the box on the floor and, when the movie's over, carry it out and put it in the trash can.

PG: Pour it over the head of the kid sitting in front of you.

R: Put it down Aunt Delia's shirt.

Now you have to go to the bathroom, but there are several people sitting in your row that you have to pass to get to the aisle. What do you do?

Invite them to come to the bathroom, too.

Climb over them.

Say quietly, "Excuse me," and go past them quickly.

The movie's over. When you get home, your aunt reminds you that you forgot to thank her for taking you. What do you say?

"I did, you didn't hear me."

"Thank you, Aunt Delia."

"I don't say thank you. That's just me."

Tricky Question 3

Which of these is the salad fork?

Playground Manners

Which is the proper way to use the water fountain?

Complete the following sentences correctly.

Aunt Delia takes you, your sister Clover, and your cousin Matt to the playground. All your friends are there. Your aunt sits down on the bench while you play freeze tag. Soon Katie comes over. When she asks, "Can I play, too?" you . . .
a) pretend you didn't hear her.
b) chant, "Skedaddle bo-battle, take your cooties to Seattle."
c) say, "Next game, you're it."

Katie joins in. She trips, chasing you. Immediately you . . .
a) help her up.
b) say, "What a klutz," and start laughing.
c) shout, "Hey, everyone, look at Katie."

Katie starts crying. That makes you feel so bad that you . . .
a) say, "Shut up, only babies cry."
b) shout, "Hey, everyone, now she's crying."
c) put your arm around her while Matt gets your Aunt Delia.

After Aunt Delia washes off Katie's knee, she buys everyone a Mister Softee. You ask for vanilla with rainbow sprinkles. Katie orders chocolate with a chocolate dip, but you . . .

a) tell her she has to have sprinkles because you say so because it's your aunt that's paying.

b) give her a lick of yours when she gives you one of hers.

c) eat so fast you get a freeze attack in your nose.

You finish your ice cream. To keep the playground clean, you . . .

a) throw the napkin in the garbage can.

b) ask Aunt Delia to vacuum.

c) bury the napkin in the sandbox.

Now Todd comes over. "Can I play, too?" he asks. You are about to say yes when Katie whispers, "Not Todd, he's creepy." So instead you . . .

a) say, "Sorry, Todd. No creeps allowed."

b) tell Katie that you like Todd and you think that if she plays with him, she will, too.

c) make fun of Todd's flat head so Katie will like you more.

After racing through sprinklers, you get into an argument about who's stayed up latest. You insist that you've stayed up until practically four in the morning. Katie doesn't believe you. To settle the argument, you . . .

a) spit at her.

b) bite her.

c) say, "You don't have to believe me, but it's true."

Then Matt comes over and says, "What's the big deal? I've stayed up all night." So you say . . .

a) "Look who's here—Big Mouth."

b) "Mind your own beeswax."

c) "Cool."

Katie says, "Isn't Matt your cousin?" And you say . . .

a) "I'm his cousin but he's not mine."

b) "Yep."

Matt does an amazing thing. He stands on his head and holds it for three minutes. Do you . . .

a) moan, "You're such a show-off"?

b) cheer, "Bravo, brambritzimel, hooray, guisunteit, villekas in the hot dog"?

Your sister Clover wants to play, too. She's four years old. "I'll be the puppy," she says. What do you do say?

"Not now, but I promise I'll play with you later."

"There are no puppies in this game, buzz off, shrimpdoodle."

"Aunt Delia, Clover's bothering us, make her stop."

Let's say you called Clover a shrimpdoodle, and Clover started crying and told Aunt Delia. "It's not nice to call anyone names," says Aunt Delia. What do you do then?

Say, "I'm sorry, Clover," and give her a hug.

Say, "I'm sorry. Just kidding. I'm not sorry, shrimpdoodle."

If you hugged Clover and apologized, what does Clover do?

Accept your applogy and hug you back.

Step on your foot

Four Playground Bonus Questions

1. Which child is misbehaving in the sandbox?

2. True or false?

You should start down a slide when another kid is still on the slide.

The best place in the playground to sit and read is at the bottom of the slide.

This is the proper way to climb the slide.

3. When you are at the top of the monkey bars, which of these things would Aunt Delia most like to hear you yell?

"I can hang from two hands."

"I can hang from one hand."

"I can hang from no hands."

4. Uncle Jerry climbs to the top to join you. In which of these conversations are you the most welcoming?

Uncle Jerry: "Hi. May I sit up here, too?"

"Get lost, bro."

"But it's a free country."

"Not for uncles."

Uncle Jerry: "Hi. Can I sit up here, too?"

"All uncles welcome. Especially you. Chill."

Bus Manners

You and Uncle Jerry are waiting for the bus. There are several people waiting with you. The bus pulls up.

Do you butt in front of everyone, shouting, "Me first, me first, me first"?

Do you fall into line without pushing or shoving?

Do you refuse to get on and demand a taxi instead?

Bus and Nose Bonus Question

As soon as you get on and sit down, you notice that the man sitting next to you has a booger hanging out of his nose.

Do you poke Uncle Jerry, point at the booger, and giggle?

Do you say to the man, "Excuse me, sir, but a booger is hanging out of your nose"?

Do you look out the window and pretend you didn't notice?

Three stops later, all the seats are taken, and an elderly couple gets on and stands in front of you and your uncle. Uncle Jerry gets right up and offers one of them his seat.

Do you get up and say to the other, "Would you like my seat"?

Do you look down and pretend you don't see them?

Your stop is next. How do you get the driver to stop?

Shout, "Stop the bus, I'm going to be sick."

Let Uncle Jerry press the buzzer.

Sing, "We're here because we're here because we're here because we're here.
We're here because we're here because we're here because we're here."

The bus pulls up to the curb. How do you get off?

Charge to the door, shouting, "Outta my way or I'll throw up on you."

Say, "Excuse me, please," as you walk to the door so that people can make room
for you to get through.

Announce, "Attention, all riders. The king of the bus is getting off here. As I
approach the door, everyone must bow and hand over five dollars."

Video Game Manners

"This is the rule," says Aunt Delia. "No video games except on weekends."

Do you scream?

Do you try to bargain, "What about if my homework's done, what about if I do my chores, what about if I wash the dog, what about if I clean the kitty litter box, what about if I practice the piano two whole extra hours"?

Do you take the game to bed and play it under the covers?

Do you hope Saturday comes soon?

Great, it's finally Saturday. Aunt Delia made pancakes. "They're ready," she calls. You are playing Super Mario. What do you do?

Stop playing and eat your breakfast.

Pour syrup on your iPad and eat the game.

Take your iPad to the table and play it while you eat.

After breakfast, your little sister wants to play My Little Pony. Aunt Delia says you should share with Clover. What do you say to Clover?

"That game is so dumb."

"I'll play for fifteen minutes and then you can play for one minute."

"Okey-doke."

Now you're playing Minecraft. Aunt Delia is watching. She says, "Do you have to kill the sheep, too? Why don't you just cut the wool?" What do you say?

"Wait until I kill this pig and then I'll explain."

"Stop talking. You just made me die."

Yikes, a zombie is coming after you. Aunt Delia says, "How was school this week, sweetie?" What is the most polite answer?

"Not now, I'm busy."

"NOT NOW, I'M BUSY!"

"May I please tell you later? I've got zombie problems."

"You just made me die."

You are getting so frustrated. You can't get to the next level.

Do you take a break?

Do you cry and scream and pull out your hair?

Now Aunt Delia wants a turn. In which of these conversations are you behaving generously and kindly?

Aunt Delia: "May I please have a turn?"

"Yes."

"I don't really know how to play."

"I'll teach you."

Aunt Delia: "May I please have a turn?"

"Beg."

"I will not. That's insulting."

"Just say, 'Pretty please.'"

"No."

"Come on, Aunt Delia. Just say those two little words and you get a turn."

"No."

"Okay. But you're just hurting yourself."

Aunt Delia: "May I please have a turn?"

You don't say anything.

"I said, 'May I please have a turn?'"

You still don't say anything.

"MAY I PLEASE HAVE A TURN?!!!"

"You don't have to shout, Aunt Delia. That's so rude. I was going to let you play, but now that you've yelled at me, you don't deserve it."

Aunt Delia: "May I please have a turn?"

"No offense, Aunt Delia, but you have to be a genius to play this."

You and Uncle Jerry are flying to Disney World. Uncle Jerry is playing iFart. Everyone on the plane can hear it. What do you do?

Ask Uncle Jerry to put on earbuds so it doesn't disturb the other passengers.

Turn the sound up louder.

Every time the game farts, try to fart, too.

When you get back from Disney World, you find out Aunt Delia has learned to play Minecraft. You play together. She explodes your house.

Do you say, "Cool move, Auntie"?

Do you throw the remote?

Facial Expression Chart

Which expressions are the most likely to get you more time for playing video games?

Which are the least likely?

Losing Manners

Your cousin Matt just beat you at Monopoly. He owns Boardwalk with two hotels, and you landed on it. Too bad. What do you do?

Throw all the money you owe him in his face.

Throw his hotels in his face.

Throw the Monopoly board in his face.

Scream, "Cheater, liar, jerk."

Say, "I guess you won, Matt. Good game."

Shopping Manners

You and Aunt Delia are entering the store as some other shoppers are leaving.

Do you shake their hands and say, "I hope you'll vote for me in November"?

Do you hold the door for them?

Do you trip them?

"What are you going to buy first, Aunt Delia?" "Perfume," she says. You follow her over to the counter. What do you do while she talks to the saleswoman?

Wait patiently.

Spray perfume on yourself and, as people walk by, say, "Smell me."

The saleswoman sprays some perfume on Aunt Delia's wrist. Your aunt invites you to sniff it. What do you say if you like it?

"Will you marry me?"

"That's a big improvement on your regular smell, Aunt Delia."

"Ooh-la-la! I like that."

Now Aunt Delia needs some new underwear, but she doesn't know where that department is. While she stands in line to pay for the perfume, you decide to help her. You go over to the information booth. What do you say?

"Hey, man, which way to the undies?"

"My aunt wants a bra size one hundred and underpants size two. Where should she go?"

"Would you please tell me where women's underwear is?"

The man informs you that women's underwear is sold on the second floor. You and Aunt Delia have to walk through the store to the escalator. She asks you to hold her hand so you don't get lost.

Do you say, "Catch me first," and run away?

Do you say, "I'm too old"?

Do you hold her hand even though you're embarrassed?

Who is riding the escalator properly?

Which of these things should you be sure to do while riding the escalator?
Pinch people's butts.
Hold on to the rail.

Now you're in women's underwear and Aunt Delia says to wait right there while she tries on some things.

Do you obey?

Do you stretch out on the floor, so shoppers have to step over you, and groan, "I'm bored. When are you going to buy *me* something"?

Do you peek in all the dressing rooms?

Your aunt does not find anything she likes, but she thanks you for being patient. "Now it's your turn," she says. "Let's go to the kids' department."

When you arrive, what do you say to the saleswoman?

"Guess what? I just saw ten naked ladies."

"I'm size eight. Bring out everything you've got and make it snappy."

"Could I please see some T-shirts and shorts, size eight?"

You select a few T-shirts and shorts to try on. Aunt Delia starts to come into the dressing room to help you, but you'd rather change in private.

Do you put a sign on the door: "Keep Out All Aunts"?

Do you let Aunt Delia in but make her face the wall while you change?

Do you say, "I'd rather try these on by myself"?

Unfortunately, nothing you try on looks good. What do you say to the saleswoman?

"All these are ugly."

"I don't think any of these is quite right. Do you have anything else?"

Now the saleswoman brings you a few more things.

Do you say, "Thank you"?

Do you say, "What's your take-home pay"?

Do you say, "Text me your number. Maybe we can meet up"?

The saleswoman peeks her head in the dressing room while you are changing and says, "How ya doing?"

Do you scream?

Do you say, "I suppose that you just heard me tell my aunt that I don't want her in here, so why in the world would I want you when we're not even related"?

Do you say, "Excuse me, but I'd like to try these on in private"?

Rats. The shirt you want costs thirty dollars. It might be too much for your aunt to spend.

Do you say, "Aunt Delia, are you too poor to buy this"?

Do you say, "It costs thirty dollars, Aunt Delia, is that too much? If it is, I'll find something else"?

Do you say, "If you really loved me, Aunt Delia, you'd buy this for me"?

On the way out of the store, your aunt discovers that the down escalator is broken. You have to take the elevator. The elevator doors open.

Do you wait until everyone gets out before getting on?

Do you announce, "This is the President of the United States with his Aunt Delia. As soon as I get inside this elevator, all passengers will please recite the Pledge of Allegiance"?

Do you dash in, yelling, "I want to push the buttons, I want to push the buttons"?

While you ride down in the elevator, what do you do?

Keep quiet.

Say, "Guess what, everyone. My aunt has a dead rat in her garage."

Put on your new T-shirt and ask everyone how they like it.

Wipe your nose on your sleeve.

Giving Compliments

You and your friend Adam are in the finals of the spelling bee. He wins after you make a mistake spelling *manners* with only one *n*. What do you say to him?

"I'm really a much better speller than you. You just got lucky."

"The judges cheated."

"All your words were easier."

"I wanted to lose."

"Congratulations."

Uncle Jerry invites you to see his
garden. He shows you his fifteen
rosebushes, all gorgeous with
flowers. "I planted these, I watered
them, I pruned them," says Uncle
Jerry proudly. What do you say?
"Big deal."
"Can I go ride my bike now?"
"They look beautiful, Uncle Jerry. You
    did a great job."

Your friend Mindy is very excited. She had a haircut and wants to show it
to you. When she arrives, you are horrified. Her hair is much too short,
especially her bangs. "How do you like my hair?" she asks. What do you
say?
"What hair?"
"It's almost right, but not quite. If you give me those
    scissors, I'll fix it."
"Don't feel bad. It'll grow."
"It looks terrific."

You asked Aunt Delia to buy you an iPod, but she said you would have to wait until your birthday to get one. Then you go over to Julie's, and she shows you what her mom just bought her—an iPod. What do you say?

"Oh, Julie, lucky you."

"That's not the good kind. The good kind has Skype, a camera, and a gazillion apps."

"If you were my friend, you'd give it to me."

"I've got something else new, too," says Julie. She takes off her jacket and shows you her cow sweatshirt. What do you say to her?

"Moo."

"Sweatshirts make you sweat and sweat makes you smell."

"It's really better if your mom or dad or aunt doesn't get you everything you want."

"Oh, I love that sweatshirt. It looks so cute on you."

"It's not fair. First you get the iPod, now the sweatshirt. I hate you."

Tricky Question 4

Who is using the soupspoon properly?

Holiday Manners

It's time to get ready to go to Thanksgiving dinner. Aunt Delia and Uncle Jerry will be there, your grandma and grandpa, your cousins Michelle, Simon, and Matt. What should you wear?

Nothing.

A tutu.

A clean shirt and pants.

Your mom says that you have to brush your hair.

Do you say, "I already did it once this week"?

Do you brush and comb it neatly?

Do you say, "I like it messy. That's the way I want it"?

After a long ride in the car, you finally arrive. Everyone is excited to see you.

Do you give Aunt Delia, Uncle Jerry, Grandma, and Grandpa a big hug and a kiss?

Do you scream, "No kisses, I hate kisses"?

Do you hug Aunt Delia and Grandma but hold your nose so you don't have to smell them?

Your grandma says, "My goodness, look how you've grown."
Do you say, "And you've shrunk"?
Do you say, "Thanks"?
Do you say, "Don't blame me. It's not my fault"?

Aunt Delia reminds you to say hello to the baby, your cousin Simon, whom you've never met because he was just born.
Do you admire him and let him hold your finger in his fist?
Do you say, "Hi, baldie, where's your hair"?
Do you say, "Hey, dude," and pass him a football?
Do you say, "Aunt Delia, don't hold him, hold me!"?

Your cousin Michelle comes downstairs to say hello. She's twelve. What do you say to her?

"What up, dawg?"

"Hi, Michelle, it's nice to see you."

"Hi, Michelle. Bye, Michelle."

Everyone sits down and Aunt Delia carries the turkey to the table.

Do you say, "Aunt Delia, that turkey looks delicious"?

Do you say, "Aunt Delia, that turkey looks mondo bizarro"?

Do you say, "What's the story, Auntie? Did you cook the cat"?

Aunt Delia asks if you want everything: turkey, cranberry sauce, creamed onions, string beans, and stuffing.

Do you say, "Nix on the stuffing, stuff the string beans in the garbage, and string the onions up a tree"?

Do you say, "Are creamed onions those little white balls floating in glue? If so, no"?

Do you say, "I'll have white meat turkey, cranberry sauce, and two string beans, please"?

Your aunt gives you your plate. On it, she put creamed onions and they are touching the turkey meat.

Do you ignore it?

Do you refuse to eat the turkey because the onions touched it?

Do you cry?

You eat some cranberry sauce and suddenly realize that it's homemade with little bits of orange rind on top. Oh, no!

Do you say, "Excuse me, Aunt Delia, but I think there are bird droppings on the cranberry sauce"?

Do you say, "I hate this kind of cranberry sauce. I like Ocean Spray in a can"?

Do you leave it on your plate and say nothing?

Do you pass your plate back and say, "Kindly get this ugly red stuff off my plate"?

Which of these are appropriate subjects for Thanksgiving dinner
conversation?

Whether the turkey knew it was going to die.

The time cousin Michelle laughed so hard while eating that a hot dog came out
of her nose.

Stink bombs.

Pilgrims.

If you wanted to make Aunt Delia really happy, which of these would you do?

Tell her you love the food.

Shout, "Food fight," and throw turkey at your cousins.

Stir the gravy with your finger.

You are finished eating before Uncle Jerry is finished carving.

Do you sit patiently and wait until everyone else has finished eating?

Do you disappear under the table and steal napkins from everyone's lap?

Do you put your head on your plate and go to sleep?

It's time to go home. What's the best way to show everyone how much you love them?

Give them each a big hug and a kiss and thank Aunt Delia for the delicious dinner.

Say, "Some Thanksgiving. The only thing I liked was the white meat turkey."

Say, "So long, Aunt Delia, Uncle Jerry, Grandma, Grandpa, Matt, Michelle, and baldie. See you at Christmas. Bring big presents."

About the Authors

Delia Ephron is a bestselling author and screenwriter. Her movies include *The Sisterhood of the Traveling Pants*, *You've Got Mail*, *Hanging Up* (based on her novel), and *Michael*. She has written novels for adults and teenagers; books of humor, including *How to Eat Like a Child*; and essays, including her most recent book, *Sister Mother Husband Dog (etc.)*. Her journalism has appeared regularly in *The New York Times*, as well as *O: The Oprah Magazine*, *Vogue*, *More*, and *Vanity Fair*. Her hit play *Love, Loss, and What I Wore* (cowritten with Nora Ephron) ran for more than two years off-Broadway and has been performed all over the world, including in Paris, Rio, and Sydney. She lives in New York City.

Edward Koren, a cartoonist and illustrator, is a regular contributor to *The New Yorker*. Among his many books are *How to Eat Like a Child* and *Teenage Romance*, both published with Delia Ephron.